DAILY
Bouquets

Helen Steiner Rice

Prayers by Virginia J. Ruehlmann

Fleming H. Revell Company
Tarrytown, New York

ISBN 0-8007-1637-X

Jacket and interior illustrations by Ed Carenza.

Bouquets to
Family, friends, and foundation trustees.
Their sincere concern for others
is a source of inspiration.

Contents

Throughout our lives, we both give and receive bouquets. We remember each bouquet because of the event that prompted the gift. We remember also the thoughtfulness of the giver.

We recall with equal joy the bouquet of wilted, yellow dandelions offered from the chubby hands of a child and an armful of freshly cut, lavender lilacs presented by a dear neighbor. We reminisce with a smile about the surprise of long-stemmed, red roses delivered by the local florist.

Floral bouquets have been used over the years to celebrate special moments: graduations, weddings, births, deaths, and holidays. But there are other types of bouquets. There are, for example, verbal and inspirational ones.

Helen Steiner Rice excelled in arranging verbal bouquets. Her poems are blossoms of comfort, peace, and love. This book is an inspirational bouquet. It combines original poems by Helen Steiner Rice, appropriate Scripture verses, and brief meditations.

It is my hope that this collection will enable you to pause and appreciate the knowledge that your life is also a bouquet, and that its blossoms are the simple and grand events, actions, and moments of each and every day.

Virginia J. Ruehlmann

Friendship's Bouquet

Life is like a bouquet
And friendship like a flower
That blooms and grows in beauty
With the sunshine and the shower.
And lovely are the blossoms
That are tended with great care
By those who work unselfishly
To make the place more fair.
And like the bouquet's blossoms
Friendships flower grows more sweet
When watched and tended carefully
By those we know and meet.
And like sunshine adds new fragrance
And raindrops play their part,
Joy and sadness add new beauty
When there's friendship in the heart.
And if the seed of friendship
Is planted deep and true
And watched with understanding,
Friendships flower will bloom for you.

Faith

"Fear not, for I have redeemed you; I have called you by name, you are mine. When you pass through the waters I will be with you; and through the rivers, they shall not overwhelm you; when you walk through fire you shall not be burned, and the flame shall not consume you."

Isaiah 43:1, 2

My cross is not too heavy,
My road is not too rough
Because God walks beside me
And to know this is enough . . .
And though I get so lonely
I know I'm not alone
For the Lord God is my Father
And He loves me as His own . . .
So though I'm tired and weary
And I wish my race were run
God will only terminate it
When my work on earth is done . . .
So let me stop complaining
About my load of care
For God will always lighten it
When it gets too much to bear . . .
And if He does not ease my load
He will give me strength to bear it
For God in love and mercy
Is always near to share it.

Almighty God, You are the source of my strength. Help me to continue even when the going is rough.

Refuge and Strength

The eternal God is your dwelling place, and underneath are the everlasting arms. . . .

Deuteronomy 33:27

> The Lord is our salvation
> And our strength in every fight,
> Our Redeemer and Protector,
> Our eternal guiding light . . .
> He has promised to sustain us,
> He's our refuge from all harms,
> And underneath this refuge
> Are the everlasting arms!

Jesus, even on the cross Your arms were spread open in welcome to me.

God's Hand

If I take the wings of the morning and dwell in the uttermost parts of the sea, even there thy hand shall lead me, and thy right hand shall hold me.

Psalm 139:9, 10

If we put our problems in God's hand,
There is nothing we need understand . . .
It is enough to just believe
That what we need we will receive.

Dear God, in the palm of Your hand I place my life. There are times when, of necessity, You will squeeze me tightly and there are other times when You will stroke me with Your tender touch. I thank You for Your interest in me.

13

In the Morning

I rise before dawn and cry for help; I hope in thy words. My eyes are awake before the watches of the night, that I may meditate upon thy promise.

Psalm 119:147, 148

I meet God in the morning
And go with Him through the day,
Then in the stillness of the night
Before sleep comes I pray
That God will just take over
All the problems I couldn't solve
And in the peacefulness of sleep
My cares will all dissolve,
So when I open up my eyes
To greet another day
I'll find myself renewed in strength
And there'll open up a way
To meet what seemed impossible
For me to solve alone
And once again I'll be assured
I am never on my own.

Loving Savior, renew my strength. Stay with me and guide me through this day. Enable me to welcome You into my life each and every morning and then when evening comes, accept my gratitude for having shared those hours with me.

Not Enough

Jesus answered him, "Truly, truly, I say to you, unless one is born anew, he cannot see the kingdom of God."

John 3:3

It's not enough to say, "I believe,"
It's not enough to ask and receive,
It's not enough to repeat the Lord's Prayer,
It's not enough to just say, "I care,"
It's not enough to be pleasant and kind,
It's not enough to keep God in your mind,
It's not enough just to feed the poor,
It's not enough to forbear and endure,
For while these things are all good to do
They cannot insure salvation for you,
For not until you are born anew
Can the Spirit of God be alive in you,
For the Spirit of God will soon be dead
Unless it is daily nourished and fed!

Father, let the Spirit of God within me be nourished daily by a spiritual menu prepared by You.

"Be brave and steadfast; have no fear or dread of them, for it is the LORD, your God, who marches with you; he will never fail you or forsake you."

Deuteronomy 31:6 NAB

The seasons swiftly come and go
And with them comes the thought
Of all the various changes
That time in flight has brought . . .
But one thing never changes,
It remains the same forever,
God truly loves His children
And He will forsake them never!

You gladden my heart, Lord, when I contemplate Your unending love. Jesus, please send a hug my way today.

"And if you obey the voice of the Lord your God, being careful to do all his commandments which I command you this day, the Lord your God will set you high above all the nations of the earth. And all these blessings shall come upon you and overtake you, if you obey the voice of the Lord your God."

Deuteronomy 28:1, 2

We are faced with many problems
  that grow bigger day by day
And, as we seek to solve them
  in our own self-sufficient way,
We keep drifting into chaos
  and our avarice and greed
Blinds us to the answer
  that would help us in our need . . .
Oh, God, renew our spirit
  and make us more aware
That our future is dependent
  on sacrifice and prayer,
Forgive us our transgressions
  and revive our faith anew
So we may all draw closer
  to each other and to You . . .

Father, thank You for the abundance of gifts that surround us. May we appreciate not only the value of natural resources of our country but also the worth of the individual families, their ideals, and their love. Keep this country and the family unit strong and God-centered. Help us to maintain the dignity and worth of each individual.

He has showed you, O man, what is good; and what
does the Lord require of you but to do justice, and to
love kindness, and to walk humbly with your God?

Micah 6:8

What must I do to insure peace of mind?
Is the answer I'm seeking, too hard to find?
How can I know what God wants me to be?
How can I tell what's expected of me?
Where can I go for guidance and aid
To help me correct the errors I've made?
The answer is found in doing three things
And great is the gladness that doing them brings . . .
Do justice, love kindness, walk humbly with God—
For with these three things as your rule and your rod
All things worth having are yours to achieve
If you follow God's words and have faith to believe!

*Heavenly Host, do not permit me to become too complacent
with the comfort of my bed and the warmth of my own
surroundings lest I forget about those who have no bed and
no home. Motivate me to take at least one small action to
help in some way.*

Climbing

Now faith is the assurance of things hoped for, the conviction of things not seen. For by it the men of old received divine approval. By faith we understand that the world was created by the word of God, so that what is seen was made out of things which do not appear.

Hebrews 11:1–3

Faith is a mover
of mountains
and there's nothing
that God cannot do,
So start out today
with faith
in your heart
and climb
till your dream
comes true!

Blessed Messiah, give me a faith so strong that I can see evidence of the gift of resurrection every day. Increase my perseverance and my determination to carry on.

Offer right sacrifices, and put your trust in the Lord.

Psalm 4:5

It's easy to say, "In God we trust"
When life is radiant and fair,
But the test of faith is only found
When there are burdens to bear—
For our claim to faith in the sunshine
is really no faith at all,
For when roads are smooth and days are bright
Our need for God is so small,
And no one discovers the fullness
Or the greatness of God's love
Unless they have waited in the darkness
With only a light from above—
So be not disheartened by troubles,
For trials are the building blocks
On which to erect a fortress of faith
Secure on God's ageless rocks.

My Rock of Strength, I trust in You. Help me accept my trials as building blocks. You have shown me the way to turn defeats into victories.

And Jesus answered them, "Truly, I say to you, if you have faith and never doubt, you will not only do what has been done to the fig tree, but even if you say to this mountain, 'Be taken up and cast into the sea,' it will be done. And whatever you ask in prayer, you will receive, if you have faith."

Matthew 21:21, 22

> Often your tasks will be many,
> And more than you think you can do . . .
> Often the road will be rugged
> And the hills insurmountable, too . . .
> But nothing in life that is worthy
> Is ever too hard to achieve
> If you have the courage to try it
> And you have the faith to believe . . .
> For faith is a force that is greater
> Than knowledge or power or skill
> And many defeats turn to triumph
> If you trust in God's wisdom and will.

With You at my side, Jesus, I believe that I can climb that insurmountable hill and travel that rugged road. Faith in You overcomes all obstacles.

Listen for God

Behold, I stand at the door and knock; if any one hears my voice and opens the door, I will come in to him and eat with him, and he with me.

Revelation 3:20

Within the crowded city . . . where life is swift and
    fleet
Do you ever look for Jesus upon the busy street?
Above the noise and laughter that is empty, cruel,
    and loud
Do you listen for the voice of God in the restless,
    surging crowd?
Do you pause in meditation upon life's thoroughfare
And offer up thanksgiving or say a word of prayer?
Well, if you would find the Savior, no need to search
    afar
For God is all around you no matter where you are.

Sometimes I think I hear You calling my name. Are You calling me, God? What would You have me do?

. . . "Great and wonderful are thy deeds, O Lord God the Almighty! Just and true are thy ways, O King of the ages! Who shall not fear and glorify thy name, O Lord? For thou alone art holy. All nations shall come and worship thee, for thy judgments have been revealed."

Revelation 15:3, 4

It's a troubled world we live in
    and we wish that we might find
Not only happiness of heart
    but longed-for peace of mind—

But where can we begin our search
    in the age of automation
With neighbor against neighbor
    and nation against nation—

Where values have no permanence
    and change is all around
And everything is sinking sand
    and nothing solid ground—

But we have God's great promise,
    so let us seek a goal
That opens up new vistas
    for man's eternal soul—

For our strength and our security
    lie not in earthly things,
But in Christ the Lord
    who died for us
And rose as King of Kings.

King of Kings, Lord of Lords, we praise You.

Prayer

In my distress I called upon the Lord; to my God I cried for help. From his temple he heard my voice, and my cry to him reached his ears.

Psalm 18:6

I have prayed in churches and chapels,
Cathedrals and synagogues, too,
But often I've had the feeling
That my prayers were not getting through,
And I realized then that our Father
Is not really concerned where we pray
Or impressed by our manner of worship
Or the eloquent words that we say . . .
He is only concerned with our feelings,
And He looks deep into our heart
And hears the cry of our soul's deep need
That no words could ever impart . . .
So it isn't the prayer that's expressive
Or offered in some special spot,
It's the sincere plea of a sinner
And God can tell whether or not
We honestly seek His forgiveness
And earnestly mean what we say,
And then and then only He answers
The prayer that we fervently pray.

Wherever I may be, let me realize that You, God, will hear me if I but lovingly call Your name.

Everything is appropriate in its own time. But though God has planted eternity in the hearts of men, even so, man cannot see the whole scope of God's work from beginning to end.

Ecclesiastes 3:11 TLB

Step by step we climb day by day
Closer to God with each prayer we pray,
For the cry of the heart offered in prayer
Becomes just another spiritual stair
In the heavenly staircase leading us to
A beautiful place where we live anew . . .
So never give up for it's worth the climb
To live forever in endless time
Where the soul of man is safe and free
To live in love through eternity!

God's stairway is open to me on my journey. Being a Christian is not an end or a final destination but rather being a Christian is a constant and endless journey in living and loving.

Two-Way Prayer

For God alone my soul waits in silence; from him
comes my salvation. He only is my rock and my salvation, my fortress. . . .

Psalm 62:1, 2

You're troubled and worried,
    you don't know what to do,
So you seek God in prayer
    and He listens to you,
But you seldom pause
    to let God speak—
You just want the answer
    that you desperately seek . . .
And you really miss
    the best part of prayer—
Which is feeling and knowing
    God's presence is there . . .
So pause for a while
    and just silently wait
And give God a chance
    to communicate,
For two-way prayer
    forms a joyous relation
When we listen to God
    in shared meditation.

*When I make a telephone call, I listen to the person on the
other end of the line. The least I can do when I call on You,
God, is to wait and listen to what You have to say. I want
to share my meditation call with You.*

Quiet Your Mind

May my meditation be pleasing to him, for I rejoice in
the Lord.

Psalm 104:34

> Brighten your day
> And lighten your way,
> Lessen your cares
> With daily prayers,
> Quiet your mind
> And leave tension behind
> And find inspiration
> In hushed meditation.

*My Blessed Messiah, help me to organize my schedule so
that I can spend some time in studying Your Word, praying
to You, and getting to know You better.*

Sure Cure

Have no anxiety about anything, but in everything by prayer and supplication with thanksgiving let your requests be made known to God.

Philippians 4:6

If your soul is sick
 and your heart is sad
And the good things in life
 begin to look bad,
Don't be too sure
 that you're physically ill
And run to the doctor
 for a sedative pill . . .
For nothing can heal
 a soul that is sick
Or guarantee a cure
 as complete and quick
As a heart-to-heart talk
 with God and His Son,
Who on the shores of the Galilee
 just said, "Thy will be done" . . .
So, when you're feeling downcast,
 seek God in meditation,
For a little talk with Jesus
 is unfailing medication.

Heavenly Physician, my prescription for today will be: Take one Bible verse and commit to memory; read the Scriptures as often as possible throughout the day; offer thanks at mealtime and before going to bed.

God's Nearness

How I love your law, O Lord!
    It is my meditation all the day.
Your command has made me wiser
        than my enemies,
        for it is ever with me.

Psalm 119:97, 98 NAB

There's a peace in meditation
Far beyond what words can say,
And in quiet contemplation
As you meditate and pray
You can feel a certain closeness
That escapes you in the crowd—
For who can hear God speaking
When life's discord cries so loud!
And free from routine pressure
    and the tensions of the day
May you enjoy God's nearness
    in a very special way.

Stay close to me, God, and increase my appreciation of Your nearness.

But rejoice in so far as you share Christ's sufferings, that you may also rejoice and be glad when his glory is revealed.

1 Peter 4:13

> Whatever your problem,
> Whatever your cross,
> Whatever your burden,
> Whatever your loss,
> You've got to believe me
> You are not alone,
> For all of the troubles
> And trials you have known
> Are faced at this minute
> By others like you
> Who also cry out,
> "Oh, God, what shall I do?"
> Just find comfort in knowing
> This is God's way of saying,
> "Come unto Me"
> And never cease praying,
> For whatever your problem
> Or whatever your sorrow
> God holds the key
> To a brighter tomorrow!

Heavenly Father, help me to recall that of all the things I wear, my expression is the most important. Permit me to meet life's trials with smiles as You and I meet the problems facing me.

Comfort

God's Appointments

For God is not so unjust as to overlook your work and the love which you showed for his sake in serving the saints, as you still do. And we desire each one of you to show the same earnestness in realizing the full assurance of hope until the end, so that you may not be sluggish, but imitators of those who through faith and patience inherit the promises.

Hebrews 6:10–12

Out of life's misery born of man's sins
A fuller, richer life begins,
For when we are helpless with no place to go
And our hearts are heavy and our spirits are low,
If we place our poor, broken lives in God's hands
And surrender completely to His will and demands,
The darkness lifts and the sun shines through
And by His touch we are born anew . . .
So praise God for trouble that cuts like a knife
And disappointments that shatter your life,
For with patience to wait and faith to endure
Your life will be blessed and your future secure,
For God is but testing your faith and your love
Before He appoints you to rise far above
All the small things that so sorely distress you,
For God's only intention is to strengthen and
     bless you.

Lord, open my eyes and help me to understand the lesson that You are trying to teach me. Everyday things seem to be getting harder to endure. Increase my endurance and my capacity to love and serve You.

Overcoming

For whatever is born of God overcomes the world; and this is the victory that overcomes the world, our faith.

1 John 5:4

If wishes worked like magic
And plans worked that way, too,
And if everything you wished for,
Whether good or bad for you,
Immediately were granted
With no effort on your part,
You'd experience no fulfillment
Of your spirit or your heart . . .
So wish not for the easy way
To win your heart's desire,
For the joy's in overcoming
And withstanding flood and fire
For to triumph over trouble
And grow stronger with defeat
Is to win the kind of victory
That will make your life complete.

Redeemer, You did not take the easy way out, nor shall I. Storms strengthen trees; so too the storms of my life will strengthen me.

When he calls to me, I will answer him; I will be with him in trouble, I will rescue him and honor him. With long life I will satisfy him, and show him my salvation.

Psalm 91:15, 16

Sickness and sorrow,
  come to us all,
But through it we grow
  and learn to stand tall . . .
And the more we endure
  with patience and grace
The stronger we grow
  and the more we can face.
And the more we can face,
  the greater our love,
And with love in our hearts
  we are more conscious of
The pain and the sorrow
  in lives everywhere,
So it is through trouble
  that we learn how to share.

Soften my sorrow, Father, and sanctify me in my distress. Grant me calmness in disappointments. May each struggle equip me to be more merciful in understanding others.

Tears

More than that, we rejoice in our sufferings, knowing that suffering produces endurance, and endurance produces character, and character produces hope, and hope does not disappoint us, because God's love has been poured into our hearts through the Holy Spirit which has been given to us.

Romans 5:3–5

Let me not live a life that's free
From the things that draw me close
    to Thee—
For how can I ever hope to heal
The wounds of others
    I do not feel—
If my eyes are dry and I never weep,
How do I know when
    the hurt is deep—
If my heart is cold
    and it never bleeds,
How can I tell what my brother needs—
So spare me no heartache
    or sorrow, dear Lord,
For the heart that is hurt
    reaps the richest reward,
And God enters the heart
    that is broken with sorrow
As He opens the door
    to a brighter tomorrow.

Heavenly Father, let my hurts and heartaches not happen in vain. Permit my experiences to teach me well so that I can be helpful to others in handling difficult circumstances and problems.

God's Tender Care

Thou who hast made me see many sore troubles wilt revive me again; from the depths of the earth thou wilt bring me up again.

Psalm 71:20

When trouble comes,
    as it does to us all
God is so great
    and we are so small—
But there is nothing
    that we need know
If we have faith
    that wherever we go
God will be waiting
    to help us bear
Our pain and sorrow,
    our suffering and care—
For no pain or suffering
    is ever too much
To yield itself
    to God's merciful touch!

Merciful Father, I need Your tender care just now. Touch my life and let me know that You are near.

Growing

The law of the Lord is perfect, reviving the soul. . . .

Psalm 19:7

May you find comfort in the thought
  that sorrow, grief, and woe
Are sent into our lives sometimes
  to help our souls to grow. . . .

For through the depths of sorrow
  comes understanding love,
And peace and truth and comfort
  sent from God above.

Father, we are all in need of growing, but sometimes it's difficult to understand the pattern of growth that You have designed for us. Help me to understand.

Jesus said to them, "I am the bread of life; he who comes to me shall not hunger, and he who believes in me shall never thirst."

John 6:35

We wouldn't enjoy the sunshine
If we never had the rain,
We wouldn't appreciate good health
If we never had a pain;
If we never shed a teardrop
And always wore a smile,
We'd all get tired of laughing
After we had grinned awhile;
Everything is by comparison,
Both the bitter and the sweet,
And it takes a bit of both of them
To make our lives complete.

My life is empty without You, Jesus. Come into my life, Lord, and make it complete. Some of Your lambs are hungry and cold. Motivate me to comfort the afflicted, to bring hope to them, to touch their lives, to feed them, to warm them. When I do for others, a completeness and a satisfaction are added to my own life.

So be truly glad! There is wonderful joy ahead, even though the going is rough for a while down here. These trials are only to test your faith, to see whether or not it is strong and pure. It is being tested as fire tests gold and purifies it—and your faith is far more precious to God than mere gold. . . .

1 Peter 1:6, 7 TLB

There are times when life overwhelms us
And our trials seem too many to bear,
It is then we should stop to remember
God is standing by ready to share
The uncertain hours that confront us
And fill us with fear and despair
For God in His goodness has promised
That the cross He gives us to wear
Will never exceed our endurance
Or be more than our strength can bear . . .
And secure in that blessed assurance
We can smile as we face tomorrow
For God holds the key to the future
And no sorrow or care need we borrow!

Dear God, may I always remember that You never close a door without opening a window for me. Refresh me with the knowledge that even in the most devastating of circumstances, You are present.

Problems

Call to me and I will answer you, and will tell you
great and hidden things which you have not known.
Jeremiah 33:3

Everyone has problems
    in this restless world of care,
Everyone grows weary
    with the cross they have to bear,
Everyone is troubled
    and their skies are overcast
As they try to face the future
    while still dwelling in the past . . .
But the people with their problems
    only listen with one ear
For people only listen
    to the things they want to hear
And they only hear the kind of things
    they are able to believe
And the answers that are God's to give
    they're not ready to receive.
But God seeks to help and watches,
    waiting always patiently
To help them solve their problems
    whatever they may be.

*Dear Lord, I want to be aware of people's problems. Develop
within me a keen sensitivity to another person's pain . . .
and let me show concern and help in some manner.*

God's Plowing

He who supplies seed to the sower and bread for food will supply and multiply your resources and increase the harvest of your righteousness.

2 Corinthians 9:10

Seed must be sown to
Bring forth the grain,
And nothing is born
Without suffering and pain
And God never plows in
The soul of man
Without intention and
Purpose and plan.

Dear God, whatever Your plan or purpose for me may be, clear my clouded heart and mind that I may see and accomplish those tasks that You desire for me to do.

I will rejoice and be glad for thy steadfast love, because thou hast seen my affliction, thou hast taken heed of my adversities.

Psalm 31:7

> The way we use adversity
> is strictly our own choice,
> For in God's hands adversity
> can make the heart rejoice—
> For everything God sends to us,
> no matter in what form,
> Is sent with plan and purpose
> for by the fierceness of a storm
> The atmosphere is changed and cleared
> and the earth is washed and clean
> And the high winds of adversity
> can make restless souls serene.

All-Wise Cornerstone of my life, blessings come in many disguises. It is my mission to unmask the adversities of life and see what blessing You have hidden within the trials that You send to me. Comforter and Counselor, energize me so that I can accept the adversities within my life.

Love

Where There Is Love

In this is love perfected with us, that we may have confidence for the day of judgment, because as he is so are we in this world. There is no fear in love, but perfect love casts out fear. For fear has to do with punishment, and he who fears is not perfected in love.

1 John 4:17, 18

Where there is love the heart is light,
Where there is love the day is bright,
Where there is love there is a song
To help when things are going wrong,
Where there is love there is a smile
To make all things seem more worthwhile,
Where there is love there's quiet peace,
A tranquil place where turmoils cease . . .
Love changes darkness into light
And makes the heart take wingless flight—
Oh, blest are they who walk in love . . .
They also walk with God above,
And when man walks with God again
There shall be peace on earth for men.

Love comes in many stages and is evidenced in many situations: a mother's love, brotherly love, the love between man and wife, the love of country . . . but the basic, and most necessary characteristic in all types of love was displayed to us by You, Dear Jesus. One can give without loving, but never can one truly love without giving.

If any one serves me, he must follow me; and where I am, there shall my servant be also; if any one serves me, the Father will honor him.

John 12:26

When someone does a kindness
    it always seems to me
That's the way God up in heaven
    would like us all to be . . .
For when we bring some pleasure
    to another human heart,
We have followed in His footsteps
    and we've had a little part
In serving Him who loves us—
    for I am very sure it's true
That in serving those around us
    We serve and please Him, too.

I want to serve You, Lord! When I help the elderly, visit the ill, and do whatever I can for the least of your brethren, am I serving You? Am I pleasing You? Am I following in Your footsteps?

The Remaining Fragrance

Cast your bread upon the waters, for you will find it
after many days.

Ecclesiastes 11:1

Flowers leave their fragrance
    on the hand that bestows them.

This old Chinese proverb
    if practiced every day
Would change the whole world
    in a wonderful way.
Its truth is so simple,
    it's so easy to do,
And it works every time
    and successfully, too.
For you can't do a kindness
    without a reward,
Not in silver nor gold
    but in joy from the Lord.
You can't light a candle
    to show others the way
Without feeling the warmth
    of that bright little ray
And you can't pluck a rose,
    all fragrant with dew,
Without part of its fragrance
    remaining with you.

Lord, fill my heart and my life with the desire to help others.
May I recognize the fact that all the joy that I put into
someone else's life eventually comes back into my own.

So faith, hope, love abide, these three; but the great-
est of these is love. Make love your aim. . . .

1 Corinthians 13:13; 14:1

> Great is the power
> of might and mind,
> But only love
> Can make us kind . . .
> And all we are
> or hope to be
> is empty pride
> and vanity . . .
> if love is not
> a part of all,
> The greatest man
> Is very small!

> Yes,
> Love is the language every heart speaks
> And love is the answer to all that man seeks.

*Father, with You directing it, love does make the world go
around. The world is like a giant symphonic orchestra. Each
one must play his or her music with no discordant notes in
order to achieve true harmony.*

Beloved, if God so loved us, we also ought to love
one another.

1 John 4:11

> Love that is shared
>   is a beautiful thing—
> It enriches the soul
>   and makes the heart sing!

*Thank You, God, for sending love into the world. Giver of
unparalleled love, I praise You. Thank You for teaching us
by being a living example of what You preached and es-
poused. Inspire me to do the same. Remind me to work with
someone and not merely give instructions, to fly kites with
my children and not just give them the kites, to walk with
my loved ones and not just point the way.*

People Need People

Do not be deceived; God is not mocked, for whatever
a man sows, that he will also reap.

Galatians 6:7

People need people
and friends need friends,
And we all need love
for a full life depends
Not on vast riches
or great acclaim,
Not on success
or on worldly fame,
But just in knowing
that someone cares
And holds us close
in their thoughts and prayers—
For only the knowledge
that we're understood
Makes everyday living
feel wonderfully good.

*Jesus, assist me to live Your truth. Encourage me to be
sensitive to the needs of others. Inspire me to offer words of
compassion, sympathy, and understanding.*

Father

Hear, my son, your father's instruction, and reject not your mother's teaching; for they are a fair garland for your head, and pendants for your neck.

Proverbs 1:8, 9

Fathers are wonderful people
    too little understood,
And we do not sing their praises
    as often as we should . . .
For, somehow, Father seems to be
    the man who pays the bills,
While Mother binds up little hurts
    and nurses all our ills . . .
And perhaps that is the reason
    we sometimes get the notion
That Fathers are not subject
    to the thing we call emotion,
But if you look inside Dad's heart,
    where no one else can see,
You'll find he's sentimental
    and as soft as he can be . . .
And like our Heavenly Father,
    he's a guardian and a guide,
Someone we can count on
    to be always on our side.

Heavenly Father, thank You for instituting the family as the most important unit in our society. Help all fathers to be responsible and to imitate You as a pattern for showing love and concern.

Mother

She opens her mouth with wisdom, and the teaching of kindness is on her tongue. She looks well to the ways of her household, and does not eat the bread of idleness. Her children rise up and call her blessed; her husband also, and he praises her.

Proverbs 31:26–28

A mother's love is something
    that no one can explain,
It is made of deep devotion
    and of sacrifice and pain,
It is endless and unselfish
    and enduring come what may
For nothing can destroy it
    or take that love away.
It is patient and forgiving
    when all others are forsaking,
And it never fails or falters
    even though the heart is breaking.
It is far beyond defining,
    it defies all explanation,
And it still remains a secret
    like the mysteries of creation.

Jesus, bless all mothers everywhere. Encourage them. Inspire them and energize them. Father is the head of the house, but Mother is the heart of the home. Help mothers and fathers to realize that the best gifts that parents can give to their children are roots *and* wings!

Anniversary

Now I will show you the way which surpasses all the others. If I speak with human tongues and angelic as well, but do not have love, I am a noisy gong, a clanging cymbal. If I have the gift of prophecy and, with full knowledge, comprehend all mysteries, if I have faith great enough to move mountains, but have not love, I am nothing. If I give everything I have to feed the poor and hand over my body to be burned, but have not love, I gain nothing.

1 Corinthians 13:1–3 NAB

This happy anniversary proves
a fact you can't disparage—
It takes true love and faith and hope
to make a happy marriage . . .
And it takes a lot of praying
and a devoted man and wife
To keep God ever-present
in their home and in their life. . . .

Father, bless all married couples. Let each partner realize that a happy and successful marriage comes not so much from finding the right partner but rather from being the right partner and demonstrating love, faith, hope, and forgiveness.

Hope

Why are you cast down, O my soul, and why are you
disquieted within me? Hope in God; for I shall again
praise him, my help and my God. . . .

Psalm 42:5, 6

When you feel cast down and despondently sad
And you long to be happy and carefree and glad,
    Do you ask yourself, as I often do,
Why must there be days that are cheerless and blue?
    Why is the song silenced in the heart this day
And then I ask God, "What makes life this way?"
And His explanation makes everything clear,
The soul has its seasons the same as the year,
Man, too, must pass through life's autumn of death
And have his heart frozen by winter's cold breath—
But spring always comes with new life and birth
Followed by summer to warm the soft earth—
And, oh, what a comfort to know there are reasons
That souls, like nature, must too have their seasons,
Bounteous seasons and barren ones, too,
Times for rejoicing and times to be blue—
For with nothing but sameness how dull life
    would be
For only life's challenge can set the soul free,
And it takes a mixture of both bitter and sweet
To season our lives and make them complete.

*Lord, whatever the season that my soul is passing through
let me appreciate You and applaud the order which You
have created for the sequence of the year. Surely, if Your eye
is on the sparrow, You will also keep watch over me in
barren or bounteous seasons of my soul.*

Smiles

When they were discouraged, I smiled and that encouraged them, and lightened their spirits.

Job 29:24 TLB

Life is a mixture of sunshine and rain,
Laughter and pleasure,
teardrops and pain,
All days can't be bright, but it's certainly true,
There was never a cloud
the sun didn't shine through—
So just keep on smiling whatever betide you,
Secure in the knowledge
God is always beside you.

*A smile can brighten not only my day but the day of those
around me. Encourage me to share my smile more often.*

Courage and Contentment

Be strong, and let your heart take courage, all you who wait for the Lord!

Psalm 31:24

God, Grant Me . . .
Courage and hope
   for every day,
Faith to guide me
   along my way,
Understanding
   and wisdom, too,
And grace to accept
   what life gives me to do.

Dear God, make me content with my station in life. Permit me to accomplish that which You have in mind for me to do but don't let me reach out for more than You want me to have.

Fresh Start

But he who looks into the perfect law, the law of liberty, and perseveres, being no hearer that forgets but a doer that acts, he shall be blessed in his doing.

James 1:25

How often we wish for another chance
    to make a fresh beginning,
A chance to blot out our mistakes
    and change failure into winning—
And it does not take a special time
    to make a brand-new start,
It only takes the deep desire
    to try with all our heart
To live a little better
    and to always be forgiving
And to add a little sunshine
    to the world in which we're living—
So never give up in despair
    and think that you are through
For there's always a tomorrow
    and a chance to start anew.

Father, train me to be a "builder-upper" of people rather than a "tearer-downer." Transfuse me with the ability to be a "doer" and not just a "hearer."

And though the Lord give you the bread of adversity
and the water of affliction, yet your Teacher will not
hide himself any more, but your eyes shall see your
Teacher. And your ears shall hear a word behind you,
saying, "This is the way, walk in it," when you turn
to the right or when you turn to the left.

Isaiah 30:20, 21

When we feel we have nothing left to give
And we are sure that the song has ended—
When our day seems over and the shadows fall
And the darkness of night has descended . . .
There's but one place to go and that is to God
And, dropping all pretense and pride,
We can pour out our problems without restraint
And gain strength with Him at our side—
And together we stand at life's crossroads
And view what we think is the end,
But God has a much bigger vision
And He tells us it's only a bend . . .
For the road goes on and is smoother,
And the pause in the song is a rest,
And the part that's unsung and unfinished
Is the sweetest and richest and best—
So rest and relax and grow stronger,
Let go and let God share your load,
Your work is not finished or ended,
You've just come to a bend in the road.

*Father, direct me on the road of life. Let me realize that
traveling life's highway can be beautiful and enriching. The
beginning and the destination depend upon me and my
attitude. Permit me to travel wisely and enjoyably.*

God Looks Inside

But the Lord said to Samuel: "Do not judge from his appearance or from his lofty stature, because I have rejected him. Not as a man sees does God see, because man sees the appearance but the Lord looks into the heart."

1 Samuel 16:7 NAB

We are often discontented
    and much dissatisfied
That our wish for recognition
    has not been gratified . . .
We feel that we've been cheated
    in beauty, charm, and brains
And we think of all our losses
    and forget all about our gains . . .
Oh, Lord, forgive our foolishness,
    our vanity, and pride
As we strive to please the eye of man
    and not God who sees inside . . .
And little do we realize
    how contented we would be
If we knew that we were beautiful
    when our hearts are touched by Thee!

Jesus, You do not dwell on my imperfections . . . Why should I? Conciliator of all mankind, reconcile me with myself. I need some self-esteem today. I realize that I must be strong. I must be conscientious. I must follow through on what has been assigned to me, but I must also remember that I must relax from time to time. Show me how! Teach me to "float awhile."

And they were exceedingly astonished, and said to him, "Then who can be saved?" Jesus looked at them and said, "With men it is impossible, but not with God; for all things are possible with God."

Mark 10:26, 27

There is no thinking person
Who can stand untouched today
And view the world around us
Slowly drifting to decay
Without feeling deep within him
A silent, unnamed dread
As he contemplates the future
That lies frighteningly ahead . . .
But his anxious fears are lessened
When he calls on God above,
For he knows above the storm clouds
Is the brightness of God's love. . . .

Dear Master, rough seas and storms will inevitably enter the course of my life. How I manage to ride through those storms will make me a better captain of my fate, my ship, and my soul.

Life's Highway

I lift up my eyes to the hills. From whence does my help come? My help comes from the Lord, who made heaven and earth.

Psalm 121:1, 2

Life is a highway
    on which the years go by . . .
Sometimes the road is level,
    sometimes the hills are high . . .
But as we travel onward
    to a future that's unknown
We can make each mile we travel
    a heavenly stepping stone!

Father, as I travel life's highway, help me to keep the road in excellent traveling condition through constant observation and necessary repairs. Assist me in observing all signals and avoiding dangerous curves and detours.

God's Great Domain

"In the sweat of your face you shall eat bread till you return to the ground, for out of it you were taken; you are dust, and to dust you shall return."

Genesis 3:19

We enter this world
    from the great unknown
And God gives each spirit
    a form of its own
And endows this form
    with a heart and a soul
To spur man on
    to his ultimate goal . . .
And man is but born
    to die and arise
For beyond this world
    in beauty there lies
The purpose of death
    which is but to gain
Life everlasting
    in God's great domain . . .
And no one need make
    this journey alone
For God has promised
    to take care of His own.

Jesus, the journey is not too long or too difficult when You are my traveling companion. When my final day comes, Lord, be with me and guide me.

Life Evermore

For as by a man came death, by a man has come also
the resurrection of the dead. For as in Adam all die,
so also in Christ shall all be made alive.

1 Corinthians 15:21, 22

We live a short while on earth below,
Reluctant to die for we do not know
Just what dark death is all about
And so we view it with fear and doubt
Not certain of what is around the bend
We look on death as the final end
To all that made us a mortal being
And yet there lies just beyond our seeing
A beautiful life so full and complete
That we should leave with hurrying feet
To walk with God by sacred streams
Amid beauty and peace beyond our dreams—
For death is only the method God chose
To colonize heaven with the souls of those
Who by their apprenticeship on earth
Proved worthy to dwell in the land of new birth—
So death is not sad . . . it's a time for elation,
A joyous transition . . . the soul's emigration
Into a place where the soul's safe and free
To live with God through eternity!

*In my journey across the bridge from here to there, let me
be encouraged by the knowledge that beyond the bend You
and my loved ones are waiting to welcome me with joyful
acclamations.*

For everything there is a season, and a time for every matter under heaven. . . .

Ecclesiastes 3:1

Who said the darkness of the night
would never turn to day,
Who said the winter's bleakness would
never pass away,
Who said the fog would never lift
and let the sunshine through,
Who said the skies now overcast would
nevermore be blue?
Why should we ever entertain
these thoughts so dark and grim
And let the brightness of our mind grow
cynical and dim
When we know beyond all questioning
that winter turns to spring
And on the notes of sorrow, new songs
are made to sing—
For no one sheds a teardrop or suffers
loss in vain,
For God is always there to turn
our losses into gain,
And every burden born today and every
present sorrow
Are but God's happy harbingers
of a joyous, bright tomorrow.

After winter has set, is spring far behind? You have created life in this same sequence. Lord, let me keep faith that the sun will come out tomorrow and that the burdens of yesterday will become the joys of today.

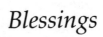

Blessings

Unexpected Miracles

Contribute to the needs of the saints, practice hospitality. Bless those who persecute you; bless and do not curse them. Rejoice with those who rejoice, weep with those who weep. Live in harmony with one another. . . .

Romans 12:13–16

The unexpected kindness
    from an unexpected place,
A hand outstretched in friendship,
    a smile on someone's face,
A word of understanding
    spoken in an hour of trial
Are unexpected miracles
    that make life more worthwhile—
We know not how it happened
    that in an hour of need
Somebody out of nowhere
    proved to be a friend indeed—
For God has many messengers
    we fail to recognize
But He sends them when we need them
    for His ways are wondrous wise!
So keep looking for an "angel"
    and keep listening to hear—
For on life's busy crowded streets
    you will find God's presence near.

Marvelous Master, teach me to take the time to be kinder. Encourage me to make the time to read a story to a child or a book to a senior citizen. When I give of myself to others, I am giving of myself to You.

Faith and Freedom

For freedom Christ has set us free; stand fast there-
fore, and do not submit again to a yoke of slavery.

Galatians 5:1

"America the Beautiful"—
May it always stay that way—
But to keep Old Glory flying
There's a price that we must pay . . .
For everything worth having
Demands work and sacrifice,
And freedom is a gift from God
That commands the highest price . . .
For all our wealth and progress
Are as worthless as can be
Without the faith that made us great
And kept our country free . . .
And "The Stars and Stripes Forever"
Will remain a symbol of
A rich and mighty nation
Built on faith and truth and love.

*Heavenly Father, let me not be complacent about our coun-
try and forget the reasons for its very founding. May I
always recall the sacrifices made in the past so that freedom
and liberty can exist in this, the present, and in the future.*

God's Presence

And he said "My presence will go with you and I will give you rest."

Exodus 33:14

The sky and the stars, the waves and the sea,
The dew on the grass, the leaves on a tree
Are constant reminders
of God and His nearness,
Proclaiming His presence
with crystal-like clearness—
So how could I think God was far, far away
When I feel Him beside me
every hour of the day,
And I've plenty of reasons to know God's my Friend
And this is one friendship
that time cannot end!

Creator God, stay near to me and allow me to see You in each beautiful act and scene of nature. Your presence is confirmed us I walk the glorious ocean beach, and my joy is increased as I observe the sand castles made by Your children at play. What wonderful gifts You have bestowed upon us!

God Whispering

... Yet he is not far from each one of us, for 'In him
we live and move and have our being'. . . .

Acts 17:27, 28

Each time you look up in the sky
Or watch the fluffy clouds drift by,
Or feel the sunshine warm and bright,
Or watch the dark night turn to light,
Or hear a bluebird gaily sing,
Or see the winter turn to spring,
Or stop to pick a daffodil,
Or gather violets on some hill . . .
Or touch a leaf or see a tree,
It's all God whispering, "This is Me . . .
And I am faith and I am light
And in Me there shall be no night."

*Dear God, if I but look, I can see signs of You. If I but
listen, I can hear evidence of You. Let me give thanks to You
for being everywhere.*

Gift of Life

When a woman is in labor she is sad that her time has come. When she has borne her child, she no longer remembers her pain for joy that a man has been born into the world.

John 16:21 NAB

A baby is a gift of life
born of the wonder of love.
A little bit of eternity
sent from the Father above.
Giving a new dimension
to the love between
husband and wife
And putting an added
new meaning
to the wonder and
mystery of life!

May I always value each stage of life, Lord. A baby is one of Your most mysterious and marvelous gifts. A baby is also proof of Your confidence in mankind and that You are willing to have this world continue!

Finding Wisdom

Happy is the man who finds wisdom, and the man who gets understanding, for the gain from it is better than gain from silver and its profit better than gold.

Proverbs 3:13, 14

Father, I have knowledge
    so will You show me now
How to use it wisely
    and find a way somehow
To make the world I live in
    a little better place,
And make life with its problems
    a bit easier to face . . .
Grant me faith and courage
    and put purpose in my days,
And show me how to serve Thee
    in the most effective ways
So all my education,
    my knowledge, and my skill,
May find their true fulfillment
    as I learn to do Thy will . . .
And may I ever be aware
    in everything I do
That knowledge comes from learning—
    and wisdom comes from You.

Father, no matter how much education I have or how many degrees I may possess, the most important fact is that You love me. The most important "degree" is the depth of that love.

And after you have suffered a little while, the God of all grace, who has called you to his eternal glory in Christ, will himself restore, establish, and strengthen you.

1 Peter 5:10

When troubles come
    and things go wrong,
And days are cheerless
    and nights are long,
We find it so easy
    to give in to despair
By magnifying
    the burdens we bear . . .
And the blessing God sent
    in a "darkened disguise"
Our troubled hearts
    fail to recognize
Not knowing God sent it
    not to distress us
But to strengthen our faith
    and redeem us and bless us.

Grapes must be crushed before the wine is made; so too, Lord, I must suffer before my faith is improved, aged, and mellowed.

Peace

. . . At that time God wrote out the Covenant—the Ten Commandments—on the stone tablets. Moses didn't realize as he came back down the mountain with the tablets that his face glowed from being in the presence of God.

Exodus 34:28, 29 TLB

Man with all his greatness
    his knowledge, and his skill,
Is still as helpless as a child
    and subject to God's will,
And there is nothing man can do
    to bring lasting joy and peace
Or curb his untamed passions
    or make his longings cease,
But the humble, full acknowledgment
    that there is no substitute
To bring forth a happy harvest
    except the Spirit's fruit
For unless man's spirit is redeemed
    he will never, ever find
Unblemished love and happiness
    and eternal peace of mind.

Dear God, redeem my spirit and help me to harvest a bountiful crop of spiritual love, a love that grows through adherence to Your Commandments. May that love nourish me as I seek eternity.

Vacation

In peace I will both lie down and sleep; for thou alone,
O Lord, makest me dwell in safety.

Psalm 4:8

We all need short vacations
 in life's fast and maddening race,
An interlude of quietness
 from the constant, jet-age pace . . .
So, when your nervous network
 becomes a tangled mess,
Just close your eyes in silent prayer
 and ask the Lord to bless
Each thought that you are thinking,
 each decision you must make,
As well as every word you speak
 and every step you take,
For only by the grace of God
 can we gain self-control
And only meditative thoughts
 can restore your peace of soul.

*Realizing that there is more to life than just work, help me,
Abba, to learn to relax a little each day and to recognize and
appreciate the humor in events around me.*

What has been is what will be, and what has been done is what will be done; and there is nothing new under the sun. Is there a thing of which it is said, "See, this is new"? It has been already, in the ages before us.

Ecclesiastes 1:9, 10

Today my soul is reaching out
For something that's unknown,
I cannot grasp or fathom it
For it's known to God alone.
I cannot hold or harness it
Or put it into form,
For it's as uncontrollable
As the wind before the storm . . .
And east and west and north and south
The same wind keeps on blowing,
While rivers run on endlessly
Yet the sea's not overflowing.
And the restless unknown longing
Of my searching soul won't cease
Until God comes in glory
And my soul at last finds peace.

Through all the ages and stages of life, Father, God, You have been present and You continue to be present. What comfort to hold on to this belief as I contemplate the mystery of life.

After the Clouds

The steadfast love of the Lord never ceases, his mercies never come to an end; they are new every morning; great is thy faithfulness.

Lamentations 3:22, 23

> After the clouds, the sunshine,
> After the winter, the spring,
> After the shower, the rainbow—
> For life is a changeable thing.
> After the night, the morning
> Bidding all darkness cease,
> After life's cares and sorrows,
> The comfort and sweetness of peace.

Loving Savior, Your faithfulness is apparent in every cloud and in each beam of sunshine. Make me steadfast in my belief that in Your mercy each sorrow will be followed by joy.

But the fruit of the Spirit is love, joy, peace, patience, kindness, goodness, faithfulness, gentleness, self-control. . . .

Galatians 5:22, 23

To be in God's keeping
is surely a blessing,
For though life is often
dark and distressing,
No day is too dark
and no burden too great
That God in His love
cannot penetrate,
And to know and believe
without question or doubt
That no matter what happens
God is there to help out,
Is to hold in your hand
the golden key
To peace and to joy
and serenity!

Holy Spirit, unlock the questions confined within my soul. Grant me discernment that I may solve the puzzle of the search for inner peace.

Your Shepherd

The Lord is my shepherd, I shall not want; he makes me lie down in green pastures. He leads me beside still waters; he restores my soul. He leads me in paths of righteousness for his name's sake.

Psalm 23:1–3

With the Lord as your Shepherd,
    you have all that you need,
For, if you follow in His footsteps
    wherever He may lead,
He will guard and guide and keep you
    in His loving, watchful care,
And when traveling in dark valleys,
    your Shepherd will be there,
His goodness is unfailing,
    His kindness knows no end,
For the Lord is a Good Shepherd
    on whom you can depend . . .
So, when your heart is troubled,
    you'll find quiet peace and calm,
If you open up the Bible
    and just read this treasured Psalm.

Heavenly Shepherd, include me in Your flock. Show me the green pastures and the still waters. Revive me. Refresh me.

Beauty and Peace

Depart from evil, and do good; seek peace, and pursue it.

Psalm 34:14

For God in His loving and all-wise way
Makes the heart that was young one day
Serene and more gentle and less restless, too,
Content to remember the joys it once knew
And all that I sought on the pathway of pleasure
Becomes but a memory to cherish and treasure—
The fast pace grows slower and the spirit serene,
And the soul can envision what the eyes have not
    seen
And so while life's springtime is sweet to recall,
The autumn of life is the best time of all,
For our wild, youthful yearnings all gradually cease
And God fills our days with *beauty* and *peace!*

If You visited my home, Jesus, would You be pleased with the manner in which I was dressed, the books on my shelf, the programs on my television? Guide me in making my life and life-style pleasing to You.

God's Care

He Cares

For the mountains may depart and the hills be removed, but my steadfast love shall not depart from
you, and my covenant of peace shall not be removed,
says the Lord, who has compassion on you.

Isaiah 54:10

Somebody cares and always will,
The world forgets but God loves you still,
You cannot go beyond His love
No matter what you're guilty of—
For God forgives until the end,
He is your faithful, loyal Friend,
And though you try to hide your face
There is no shelter any place
That can escape His watchful eye,
For on the earth and in the sky
He's ever present and always there
To take you in His tender care
And bind the wounds and mend the breaks
When all the world around forsakes . . .
Somebody cares and loves you still
And God is the Someone who always will.

*Ever-present Father, what comfort, what solace, what con-
solation, and what relief to know that You care for me.*

Say to those who are of a fearful heart, "Be strong, fear not! Behold, your God will come with vengeance, with the recompense of God. He will come and save you." Then the eyes of the blind shall be opened, and the ears of the deaf unstopped; then shall the lame man leap like a hart, and the tongue of the dumb sing for joy. . . .

Isaiah 35:4–6

Prayers for big and little things
Fly heavenward on angels' wings—
And He who walked by the Galilee
And touched the blind and made them see,
And cured the man who long was lame
When he but called God's holy name,
Will keep you safely in His care
And when you need Him He'll be there!

Holy Father, keep me aware of Your presence every day and in every way.

Strong in His Love

He who dwells in the shelter of the Most High, who abides in the shadow of the Almighty, will say to the Lord, "My refuge and my fortress; my God, in whom I trust."

Psalm 91:1, 2

"Love Divine, All Loves Excelling"
Makes my humbled heart Your dwelling,
For without Your love divine
Total darkness would be mine,
My earthly load I could not bear
If You were not there to share
All the pain, despair, and sorrow
That almost makes me dread tomorrow . . .
But somehow when I realize
That He who made the sea and skies
And holds the whole world in His hand
Has my small soul in his command,
It gives me strength to try once more
To somehow reach the heavenly door
Where I will live forevermore
With friends and loved ones I adore!

My Dear God, my strength is derived from You. May I never forget the Source of my strength and may Your strength sustain me and stay with me always in all ways.

The Master Builder

For we are fellow workers for God; you are God's field, God's building. According to the grace of God given to me, like a skilled master builder I laid a foundation, and another man is building upon it. Let each man take care how he builds upon it. For no other foundation can any one lay than that which is laid, which is Jesus Christ.

1 Corinthians 3:9–11

God is the Master Builder,
His plans are perfect and true,
And when He sends you sorrow
It's part of His plan for you . . .
For all things work together
To complete the master plan
And God up in His heaven
Can see what's best for man.

Master Builder, a carpenter is known for his building skills. I pray that You build me into whatever plan You have in mind.

Growing Older

Do not cast me off in the time of old age; forsake me not when my strength is spent.

Psalm 71:9

You can't hold back the dawn
Or stop the tides from flowing—
Or keep a rose from withering
Or still a wind that's blowing—
And time cannot be halted
In its swift and endless flight
For age is sure to follow youth
Like day comes after night . . .
For He who sets our span of years
And watches from above
Replaces youth and beauty
With peace and truth and love . . .
And then our souls are privileged
To see a hidden treasure
That in our youth escaped our eyes
In our pursuit of pleasure . . .
So birthdays are but blessings
That open up the way
To the everlasting beauty
Of God's eternal day.

Heavenly Father, let me speak with respect and consideration to those older than I. As I, myself, grow older, permit me to keep my enthusiasm and zest for living and not emphasize the number of years lived but the joys of the experiences gained through the years.

Enfolded by Love

As the Father has loved me, so have I loved you;
abide in my love. If you keep my commandments,
you will abide in my love, just as I have kept my
Father's commandments and abide in his love. These
things I have spoken to you, that my joy may be in
you, and that your joy may be full.

John 15:9–11

The love of God
surrounds us
like the air
we breathe around us—
As near
as a heartbeat,
as close as a prayer,
And whenever
We need Him
He'll always be there!

Each breath I take, each beat of my heart, each prayer I say,
my Loving Savior, You are a part.

I cry aloud to God, aloud to God, that he may hear
me. In the day of my trouble I seek the Lord. . . .

Psalm 77:1, 2

God help us to accept Your love
    that You offer us for free
And make us ever thankful
    that You give it lavishly
But make us also conscious
    that Your love comes in many ways
And not always just as happiness
    and bright and shining days
But often You send trouble
    and we foolishly reject it
Not realizing that it is Your will
    and we should joyously accept it
And in trouble and in gladness
    we can always hear your voice
If we listen in the silence
    and find a reason to rejoice.

*Dear God, You answer all my prayers in Your own way
and in Your own timing, but always Your answer is given
with mercy and love.*

"He will wipe away all tears from their eyes, and there shall be no more death, nor sorrow, nor crying, nor pain. All of that has gone forever."

Revelation 21:4 TLB

God, how little I was really aware
Of the pain and the trouble and deep despair
That floods the hearts of those in pain
As they struggle to cope but feel it's in vain,
Crushed with frustration and with no haven to seek,
With broken spirits and bodies so weak . . .
And yet they forget Christ suffered and died
And hung on the cross and was crucified,
And He did it all so some happy day,
When the sorrows of earth have all passed away,
We who have suffered will forever be free
To live with God in eternity!

Diminish my hesitancy to reach out to others. Expand the confines of my caring. There are many who need me, God.

I consider that the sufferings of this present time are not worth comparing with the glory that is to be revealed to us.

Romans 8:18

I wish I could wipe away every trace
Of pain and suffering from your face
But He is great and we are small
We just can't alter His will at all

And none of us would want to try
For more and more, as days go by,
We know His plan for us is best
And He will give us peace and rest

And earthly pain is never too much
If He has bestowed His merciful touch
And if you look to Him and pray
He will help you through every day.

If there was no pain or sorrow, how could I ever learn to call upon You, Father, with faith in my heart?

Serving Him

"... but whoever would be great among you must be your servant, and whoever would be first among you must be your slave; even as the Son of man came not to be served but to serve, and to give his life as a ransom for many."

Matthew 20:26–28

Now, the earth is where we live today
And we must serve God here,
For He watches us from way up there
And His love is always near. . . .

Father, guard my comments. Let me strive to maintain the dignity of each and every individual at home, at work, at school, at play . . . wherever I may go.

God's Love

. . . "The Lord is my rock, and my fortress, and my deliverer, my God, my rock, in whom I take refuge, my shield and the horn of my salvation, my stronghold and my refuge, my savior; thou savest me from violence."

2 Samuel 22:2, 3

God's love is like an island
In life's ocean vast and wide—
A peaceful, quiet shelter
From the restless, rising tide . . .

God's love is like an anchor
When the angry billows roll—
A mooring in the storms of life,
A stronghold for the soul . . .

God's love is like a harbor
Where our souls can find sweet rest
From the struggle and the tension
Of life's fast and futile quest . . .

God's love is like a beacon
Burning bright with faith and prayer
And through the changing scenes of life
We can find a haven there!

Dear God, You are my anchor in the storms of everyday living. Keep me afloat and prevent me from drifting away from You.

And I will walk among you, and will be your God,
and you shall be my people.

Leviticus 26:12

You are young and life is beginning
in a wonderful way for you,
The future reaches its welcoming hand
with new, challenging things to do.
And here is a prayer for you
that you'll walk with God every day,
Remembering always in whatever you do
there is only one true, righteous way—
For God in His wisdom and mercy
looked down on His children below
And gave them the privilege of choosing
the right or the wrong way to go . . .
So trust in His almighty wisdom
and enjoy the fruit of His love—
And life on earth will be happy
as you walk with the Father above.

*Heavenly Father, guide me in choosing the right way every
day and help me to remember that there is never a right way
to do a wrong act.*

For Christ also died for sins once for all, the righteous
for the unrighteous, that he might bring us to God,
being put to death in the flesh but made alive in the
spirit.

1 Peter 3:18

From Bethlehem's manger
    to Calvary's Hill
This sinless Savior
    and Man of goodwill
Changed our lives
    for, by His birth,
He brought God's love
    from heaven to earth—
He dwelled among men
    and He lived and died,
And for man's sins
    He was crucified
How can we deny
    this Man of goodwill
Who died for us all
    on Calvary's Hill.

*Jesus, You not only carried the cross on Your shoulders but
You continue to carry the weight of the world. Please save
enough room to carry me and my problems.*

If you found any beauty in the poems of this book
Or some peace and comfort in a word or line
Don't give me praise or worldly acclaim
For the words that you read are not mine . . .
I borrowed them all to share with you
From our Heavenly Father above,
And the joy that you felt was God speaking to you
As He flooded your heart with His love.

H.S.R.

And if you receive hope or strength
From the Scripture or from the prayer
Know that whenever or wherever you read this,
Our Heavenly Father is there!

V.J.R.